Growing up at Papa and Nonna's House

Beth Caparelli

Copyright © 2023
Beth Caparelli

Dedications

This book was inspired and written for my beautiful granddaughter

Acknowledgments

To my English professor in college requiring we write a book as our final project. To my husband for encouraging me to publish this book.

About the Author

Beth Caparelli grew up in New England. She still resides in New England with her husband of 44 years. She has two daughters and four grandchildren.

She attended the Community College of Rhode Island, where she received a degree in accounting. She then went on to Johnson & Wales University to earn a master's degree in business with a concentration in accounting. She works as a controller for an international manufacturing company and as an adjunct professor for the Community College of Rhode Island. She loves teaching and hopefully making a difference in the student's future and spending Sunday dinners with her family.

Growing Up At Papa and Nonna's House

This is my story about growing up at Papa and Nonna's house. First, I would like to introduce my family.

My mom's name is Samantha. My dad's name is Jay. Papa's name is Sal, and Nonna's name is Beth. And my name is Natalia Lynn.

Nonna				Papa

My mom and dad chose the name Natalia because I was born during the Christmas holiday. Nonna and Dad were with Mom when I was born. Papa was patiently waiting for the news of my arrival.

The day came to leave the hospital. We all went to live at Papa and Nonna's house. I had my own room. I love my new home.

I was always very excited to see everyone come home from work. I would hide until they found me. We would have dinner together.

After dinner, Papa would take me outside and push me on my swing. In the fall, Papa would rake the leaves in a pile for me to jump in. As I got older, we would make pizza together. I love my home.

Nonna and I would play with my dolls and pretend we were sisters.

At bedtime, Nonna would read me a book and help put me to bed. I love my home.

NOW I LAY me DOWN TO SLeep

One day Mom and Dad said we were moving to our own home. I was very upset about moving. This was my home.

Moving Company

I love my home and being with Papa and Nonna. When will I see them? I started to cry. The day came, and we did move to our new home. I was very sad.

Every Sunday, we visit with Papa and Nonna and have dinner together. I see them when I sleep over on Friday night. We have a special time together.

I now realize that it is okay to live in a different home. We are all very happy, and now I have a new baby brother. His name is Collin. All is okay. But, I still love Papa and Nonna's house.

www.ingramcontent.com/pod-product-compliance
Lightning Source LLC
Chambersburg PA
CBHW041215240426
43661CB00012B/1047